WITHDRAWN LOW-MAINTENANCE GARDENS

Published in Great Britain in 2008
by John Wiley & Sons Ltd

Other Wiley Editorial Offices

John Wiley & Sons Inc., 111 River Street, Hoboken,
NJ 07030, USA

Jossey-Bass, 989 Market Street, San Francisco,
CA 94103-1741, USA

Wiley-VCH Verlag GmbH, Boschstr. 12,
D-69469 Weinheim, Germany

John Wiley & Sons Australia Ltd, 42 McDougall Street,
Milton, Queensland 4064, Australia

John Wiley & Sons (Asia) Pte Ltd, 2 Clementi Loop #02-01,
Jin Xing Distripark, Singapore 129809

John Wiley & Sons Canada Ltd, 5353 Dundas Street West,
Suite 400, Etobicoke, Ontario M9B 6H8, Canada

Wiley also publishes its books in a variety of electronic
formats. Some content that appears in print may not be
available in electronic books.

Executive Commissioning Editor: Helen Castle
Project Editor: Miriam Swift
Publishing Assistant: Calver Lezama

ISBN 978-0-470-51751-2

Cover photo © Steve Gorton

Cover design © Jeremy Tilston, The Oak Studio Limited

Photo credits
All photographs by Steve Gorton unless stated below:
pp 20, 31 (b), 36 (b), 44 (t), 47 (t) © The Garden Trellis
Company Ltd

Page design and layouts by
Jeremy Tilston, The Oak Studio Limited
Prepress by Artmedia Press Ltd • London
Printed and bound by Printer Trento, Italy

Low-Maintenance Gardens

Garden Style Guides

CAROLINE TILSTON

Photography by Steve Gorton

LOW-MAINTENANCE GARDENS

INSPIRATION

Introduction

Why talk about low maintenance gardens? Would anyone talk about a low-maintenance dining room or bedroom? I've never heard of it. When people talk about rooms inside the house there are so many other things to focus on making the most of the space, exciting colours, lighting, great furniture. You assume these rooms need a dust and a hoover every week or so and a new lick of paint every so often, but that goes without saying. Maintenance is taken as part of life, like washing your clothes or doing the dishes. So why are people (OK, books like this one!) so keen on making an issue of low-maintenance gardens? What's the difference between an inside room and an outside one? *Plants*.

They cause stress about which ones to put in, they grow and take over, or worse, don't grow and die. They need watering and feeding, and all of a sudden it's like having a pet rather than having a room outside.

The logical conclusion from this is that if you remove all the plants the garden will be no higher or lower maintenance than any other room, and we can move on and talk about positive and exciting things like decoration and design.

But, very rarely do people want to remove all plants from the garden. It seems somehow not to be a garden if it doesn't have any plants at all.

And this is where the fodder for books like this comes in – what can you have in your garden keeping it as close to normal 'room maintenance' as possible?

What about a lawn?
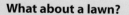
If you think of this as a carpet that needs a vacuum once a week (using a lawn mower rather than the Dyson) it might be acceptable. If that's too boring you can pull the lawn up, replace it with paving and it'll just need a sweep. Rather like pulling the carpets up inside the house and revealing the floorboards.

Containers?
Well they're like houseplants and no one worries about having to remember to water them, they seem very … 'contained' and controllable.

Planted beds?

Now this is where we start to get into gardening, pure and simple, and this is where people who don't want to do gardening switch off. It may be possible to remove all the planted beds and there are plenty of gardens that do just that. A halfway house between planted beds and containers is raised beds – they still seem quite controllable and can be called large containers if you stretch it – and you might be happy to have a few bits of 'real gardening' in there if the plants are as self-sufficient as possible.

So this book will talk about these and how to include them in the garden and keep the work down to a minimum.

I really want to break away from the negative feel of most books on low-maintenance gardens. They always remind me of diet books – counting minutes spent in the garden like counting calories – when really we should be celebrating how wonderful gardens can look even when … no, *especially* when there's not too much gardening to do.

Gardens are rooms outside yes, but they are so much more exciting than just another room. You have much wider scope for creating your own world and for letting your imagination run riot.

I happen to think gardens are more exciting than anything inside the house because the possibilities for creating spaces and for changing them are so much greater; but fundamentally, the similarities between outside and in outweigh the differences. Once I've finished talking about the really time-consuming 'gardening' tasks and how to design them out of your garden, what I'm focusing on is creating really exciting spaces. Yes, they'll need a dust and a brush every week or so, but no more and no less than the dining room.

So we've a little in here that's a bit negative – about taking out and reducing and compromising – but most of the book, and by far the most important part, is about inspiration for what can be achieved outside.

So the approach of the book is ...

1. Planning

Plan to remove as much gardening as you can and as you want to from your garden.

2. Design

Design it to be stunning with or without the green stuff.

3. Horizontals

Once you've got the design, what to make the floor out of.

4. Verticals

And how to form the uprights – walls, fences, hedges.

5. Plant design

If you do put plants in the garden I've included a section on how to do it as painlessly as possible.

6. Which plants?

And then a directory of which plants to use.

7. Lighting

Lighting and making the best use of light in the garden.

8. Water

Strictly not low maintenance – water will take a bit of cleaning and tinkering, but it's not really gardening.

9. Decoration

What are the best decorations?

10. Wildlife

A wildlife garden can be wonderfully low maintenance; it's an off-the-wall solution to the maintenance problem.

After that there are 10 wonderfully inspirational, low-maintenance gardens to look at.

SOMETHING TO THINK ABOUT ...

An interesting side note is that many gardens by top designers will be low maintenance. People who are keen gardeners tend not to get designers in, so part of most briefs to designers will be to make the garden 'low maintenance'. Which means that the real cutting-edge garden design, the brilliant, exciting new trends, come into this category.

Planning

To get to the garden you want there is a logical process to go through – information gathering and decision making. It starts by looking at what you've got, what you like, what you don't like.

Stage 1

What don't you like about the garden ...

When the aim is to make a garden lower maintenance a lot of this is going to be looking at the jobs you don't like doing and making a note to remove whatever is causing the work you don't like.

But there may also be other things you don't like about the garden – it may be dull in winter, there may be nowhere to sit, it may just be boring.

If you've just moved in to a property it is worth living with a garden for a while to get to know all of this and to watch the light move and to see how you use the garden naturally. The purpose of some things may become more apparent after a time – a tree that looks in the wrong place may be hiding a bad view or helping to give shelter from a cold wind.

New houses – what's not to like?

You might be able to skip this stage if you've got a new property and a blank canvas. There may not be anything there to dislike, so the process pretty much begins at stage two – writing down what you would like from your garden.

Lighting – look at ...

1. Where the sunlight is at different times of the day – so you know where to put the shady seat and the sunny seat.

2. Where the sunlight is at different times of the year. If your garden is north facing, in high summer when the sun is overhead you may be OK, but come September you'll quickly lose all direct light as the arc of the sun gets lower and lower behind your house.

Want to remove a tree?

Be very careful when you are thinking about taking out trees. They give such character to a garden and the sort of maturity that can't be replaced easily. Before you go ahead and remove a tree altogether think about taking off the bottom branches and raising its canopy. If you really have to get rid of a tree, always check with the local council that there are no restrictions on the area or the tree.

It is amazing how often the same things arise in gardens that annoy or irritate or just befuddle people. I've put a list of the most common problems below. Having said that, there are usually a few additional things that are entirely personal to you and your garden.

As well as the problem I've put a few solutions down, this shows how these problems will translate into action on the ground.

Problem

Solution

Cutting the lawn

This takes time especially if it's a tricky shape with lots of odd corners; a lawn that's shady and/or in poor condition. Reshape, re-lay the lawn or remove it altogether.

Completely overgrown garden

Cut it back, don't worry about the plants – it's your garden and if you can't use it then it's no use to anyone.

A pond or water feature that's always going wrong

Lose it if you can – fill it in or pull it out. If you really want to keep it it's probably worth getting specialist advice to fix it properly and make it low maintenance for the future.

High hedges that are difficult to cut

Take the height of the hedges right down to a height that's easier to maintain, or pull them up and replace with something slower growing or a fence or wall if necessary.

Problem	Solution
Vegetable plot	If you want a low-maintenance garden the answer is to lose it. Turn it into a sitting area or pave it. If you want to grow vegetables it's easier, in a lot of ways, to use containers.
Small containers which need constant watering	Larger containers will be easier so replace them if you can, but if you want to keep the small ones at least put them all together in one place. It makes them easier to water and keep an eye on (and they look better that way).
Hanging baskets	These are incredibly high maintenance and logically they ought to be out on their ears, but ... do you really not like them? Lots of people with a complete aversion to gardening have a soft spot for these.

Stage 2

We've dealt with the negatives, the things you don't like in the garden, now the positives. What do you want, like and need from the garden?

Let's assume you want a low-maintenance garden, given that you're reading this book!

As well as the things that you want I've also put down a few of the solutions to the wants – so you can see how they might end up in the garden.

Storage

There's more to storage than sheds

You don't have to have a shed, it may be just too big. Think about exactly what it is you need to store – it might just be a spade and a hammer – and then choose the size of your storage to fit. Available off the peg are seats with storage underneath, tall units to fit into tiny corners, low boxes that will fit under windows. It's worth looking on the Internet to see what's available. Often putting something right next to the house, even under a window, is a great solution, so you don't see it when you look out from the house. It also means that things are very accessible and probably more secure than further down the garden such as these beautiful storage units from The Garden Trellis Company.

Want	Design solution
Some greenery	In a low-maintenance garden you might not want plants at all, but if you do there are plenty of low-maintenance options. See Chapters 5 and 6 – plant design and choice.
Changes with the seasons and winter interest	It's relatively easy to have a garden with greenery that stays pretty much the same all year round. If you want changes through the year it takes careful thought but it is possible.
Access to the rear of the garden	If this is used a lot and throughout the year you will need hard surfaces to walk on, but the path doesn't have to be a single straight line going to the back, it can be stepping stones or part of a wider area of paving or gravel.
Raised beds	These are really useful if you have a small garden dominated by its fences or walls. The raised beds help to decrease the visible height of the walls and break up the lines. They also seem really contained and much more manageable to look after.
A water feature	Even if you want low maintenance you might still want water. Generally these do take a little tinkering but if it's something you want, you understand and are happy to do, it won't seem like work.
Something really stunning	This is where the fun begins; you can really go to town in a garden and use colour and shapes to make a stunning space.
Lighting	Lighting will help to make a space exciting after nightfall and is pretty low maintenance.
Neat	It's worth thinking about how neat you are or how much mess you can tolerate or enjoy. This will have a huge effect on the type of garden you will be happy with. In a nutshell a messy person will find it easier to have a low-maintenance garden. If you can't tolerate dirt and weeds, planning needs to be more fastidious.

So now you know what you've got and what you want it's time to see what design might be good for you.

Design

Whether you're starting from a blank canvas or remodelling an existing garden it's worth thinking about the overall design. Changing the composition rather than tinkering around the edges is always going to be the most effective way of making a low-maintenance garden – so you take control of how it works for you.

How to design — in one easy, low-maintenance step ...

The first, last and only unbreakable rule of garden design ...

Create spaces, create rooms. Don't let the living spaces within the garden be tied to the overall shape of it. When I teach garden design the first thing people will do is something like this ... They are putting into the garden the things they want and need, but not thinking about the design.

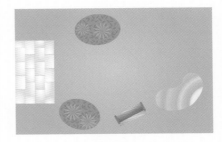

This is a design. Rooms which will be beautiful to sit in have been made. The same things are in the same places – but they've been organised into a coherent whole.

Making shapes on the ground

So to make the rooms you put good strong shapes on the ground. I think this is the fun bit of design – thinking about which shapes, what types of rooms will work in your garden. If you have a blank canvas you'll have more choice, if you need to accommodate things that are already there, you may be more limited in which ones you could go with.

TIP

The stronger the lines of the garden's design, the more you will get away with if you let the grass grow or don't quite remember to do the weeding.

15 ways to divide a standard garden
Square, triangle, rectangle

Don't let the shapes go too close to the edges of the garden – these spaces will probably be planted and you need room to put something there.

Most of these designs have a patio at one end. You may need a patio right next to the house – but it doesn't have to be there.

Sitting in a long thin shape doesn't feel right – so here the garden is broken down into rooms with better proportions.

Squares are pretty nice shapes to be in anyway so you can just use the shape of the garden – but make sure the walls are given some unity, maybe with battens or trellis.

Triangular gardens are great to design; they can be transformed beyond recognition just by demarcating different shapes within the boundaries.

Think outside the box ...

When you're dividing up the space, you don't have to decide immediately what each shape or area will be formed by. The circle in the middle might be lawn – but it could be something else like gravel or stone. It's worth remembering: the more hard landscaping you have – the fewer the plants – the lower the maintenance.

Measuring and planning

You don't have to do a plan on paper, walking around the garden and marking things out on the ground will work just as well; and, if you have a lot of stuff in the garden already and are just tinkering, it will be a lot easier to mark changes on the ground than trying to plot everything onto paper. Line paint from a builders' merchant is ideal to draw things out on grass and soil, but if it goes on paving it's a pain to get off. Or you can just use string and stakes to demarcate areas.

But if you can do a scale plan of the garden and mark on it all the existing features that need to stay it will mean you can experiment more with different shapes and ways to divide the space up. Make lots of photocopies of the plan and have a play.

Sun or shade?

Quite apart from any maintenance issues, sun and shade are incredibly important in gardens and it's good to get to know where they fall during the day and at different times of the year. You may want to sit in the sun or in the shade; you may want children's play equipment to be in the shade. If you can't decide whether you want a sitting area in the sun or shade, put it in the sun, you can always bring in shade.

Checklist for a low-maintenance garden

- **Adequate storage and a place to put rubbish**
- **Washing line near to the house**
- **Paths around the garden**
- **Paved areas for seating**
- **As much gravel, decking, paving as possible**

Once you've worked out the shapes, the rooms, the next thing to decide is – what will make those shapes, how will the divides be created.

Horizontals
Floors & Lawns

Once you have the design marked out, either on paper or on the ground, the next thing to do is to decide how the shapes will be formed and how the divides and surrounds, the verticals, will be made. Starting with the horizontals.

As far as low-maintenance gardens are concerned, whether to have a lawn or not is an incredibly important decision. If you want low maintenance you really ought to get rid of the lawn and put hard landscaping over everything, but it's not always as easy as that.

Lawn

To have a lawn or not

One of the biggest choices – both in terms of spending money and spending time – will be what to have on the ground. Paving is expensive but easy to look after; grass is cheap to put in but relatively high maintenance.

FOR AND AGAINST LAWNS

For

- You would have to put something down and the alternatives are generally more expensive
- Easy to lay
- Grass seed is very inexpensive, turf slightly more expensive, but still cheaper than paving
- It's green all year round
- Great for children to play on

Against

- Needs mowing every week and yearly maintenance
- Smaller gardens tend to have shaded areas so grass grows really badly
- In areas of high use the grass gets worn very quickly
- There are loads of choices with paving, grass is just green
- Maintenance couldn't be easier with paving – just a brush and it's done
- Garden chairs tend to sink into it
- Lawns tend to go centrally in the garden and so dictate the design – with plants around and paths down the side; lose the lawn and many more options become available
- Can be unusable in winter

Perhaps the easiest option is a good old fudge – cut down the amount of lawn, simplify its shape, increase the amount of expensive paving and fill in the rest with low-maintenance planting.

If you don't have a lawn the alternative doesn't have to be boring. This sculptural timber floor with inset stones and box balls was designed by Aurélien Liutkus and built by Mark Wallinger Landscapes. Ipe hardwood was supplied by the Garden Trellis Company.

Making lawns easier

So if you do keep the lawn but still want to keep the maintenance down look very hard at the shape of it and how it's accessed.

1. Easy shape

If possible create the overall shape of the lawn with your lawnmower – actually take the mower around and make any curves with it on the ground. That way there won't be any awkward corners or strange little bits.

TIP

This is one of garden designers' greatest secrets. If you make a good strong shape to the lawn – fill in what's left with paving and planting – you've pretty instantly got a good design.

2. Keep it clear

Avoid having anything within the lawn if at all possible. Certainly avoid little things dotted here and there like shrubs, seats or ornaments. These will be a pain to mow around or move every time. If there's a tree or something that you can't move, make a good large shape around it that's easy to navigate with the mower and either leave the grass within that shape uncut or create an island bed of plants around it.

3. Mowing edge

A mowing edge, a strip of hard landscaping all around the lawn, will help to make the lawn easier to mow – you won't be bumping into overhanging flowers at the edges.

4. No verticals right next to lawn

Always try to avoid a lawn going straight to an upright, it's difficult to try and cut the grass right up to a fence or wall. Even if you just put down a line of cobbles or gravel around the edges it will help you run the mower over the edge of the grass.

5. Heights of horizontals

Make sure the lawn is higher than anything surrounding it – gravel, cobbles, paving, soil – so you can run the mower right over the edge.

6. Storing the mower

Try to have the mower very near the lawn and try to make sure you don't have to negotiate any steps or other obstacles getting the mower to the lawn and back.

If your grass is really long ...

Try not to leave the lawn too long between cuts. If you cut more than a third off the height, the grass will not be happy and will probably turn brown. If you have left it too long and really need to cut a lot off, try to do the cut when there's the best chance of the lawn recovering, with lots of rain, sun and warmth. If these are present the grass can start growing and greening up again.

Keeping lawn care to a minimum

1. Moss and weeds can cause work if you want to get rid of them, but you can just live with them. I live with the moss, daisies and buttercups in my lawn as I think the effort to try and get rid of them just isn't worth it – they're quite pretty and green.

2. Most weeds don't, unlike grass, tolerate having their tops cut off regularly. So regular mowing will get rid of a lot of weeds.

3. Every time you cut the lawn you take nutrients away from the plants. It's worth, every once in awhile, putting some food back. The easiest way I've found is pelleted chicken manure; you can buy a big tub of it from most DIY shops. Twice a year, spring and autumn, I chuck it about the lawn. Downside – it smells a bit for a few days, so don't do it just before a big barbie.

THE BEST OF BOTH WORLDS

No maintenance, easy to lay, inexpensive, green all year around. Three garden designers have admitted to me in the past few months that they are putting in fake grass. It's worth a look.

The grass in this lawn is LazyLawn™ by Evergreens UK Limited.

The hard stuff

If you're going for low maintenance, more is better as far as hard landscaping is concerned. However it will be more expensive.

Top tips for making hard landscaping work

1. Essentially it's a very practical element of the garden – is it going to work for you?
2. Don't mix too many different types of surfaces together.
3. The lowest maintenance tend to be the most expensive – stone, pavers and concrete blocks. The less expensive things tend to rely on a bit more housework from you – decking, gravel, bark chips.

Decking

- It's great for creating a flat area on uneven ground; the lengths of the uprights can be varied to give a really good level surface.
- This is especially important in a small garden that slopes down, away from the house. Decking can be a godsend here, creating a usable space for tables and chairs.
- It can save a lot of time and effort if you're laying decking over an existing old patio – there's no need to pull up the old stones, they will be a good base for the wood.
- You can paint it but it will need regular maintenance, as the paint will chip.
- There are lots of wonderful lights available which can be set into the

wood. Coloured LED spots can create great effects.

- You can create a curve but it's difficult and often doesn't look very good – better to stick to straight edges.
- Hardwood will be the longest lasting and lowest maintenance.
- Decking boards also come in pre-made squares.
- You can cut a hole in the deck and plant a tree or tall plants through the decking.
- Always enclose the deck and surround it with plants.
- Try to have planting between the deck and any uprights like walls or fences. If this isn't possible at least put some long low troughs along the back to help break up the hard surfaces.
- Decking can be made on more than one level.
- Built-in seats of the same wood can look wonderful.

Fairly easy to do and it makes decking so much more interesting – create a circle and plant a tree through the deck. This deck was made by the Garden Trellis Company.

Gravel

- Gravel is pretty much the cheapest type of hard landscaping to buy and the easiest to lay.

- Light-coloured gravel is great at reflecting the light and giving a good foil to the plants.

- For a weed-free gravel path make sure it has a semi-permeable membrane underneath (or just cheat and spray with Pathclear once a year).

- There are different types of gravel, different sizes, and different colours. It's worth going to a builders' merchant to look at all the different types. For example, shingle is made of small chips and pea shingle has rounded edges. Then there are all the quartzite, slates and cobbles …

- Some people really don't like gravel – the kids eat it, the cats poo in it and it gets kicked everywhere. Two solutions:

- Only lay a very shallow skim of gravel, most people put their gravel in too deep, so you almost end up swimming through it.

- Or use bound gravel or self-binding gravel. The former sticks the gravel to a surface (something like resin) underneath; the latter is rolled so the gravel isn't loose.

Bark chips

You can use these like gravel as the surface for a path or area.

- It is particularly good for children's play areas; it makes a relatively soft landing.
- It is great for woodland-like paths.
- You will have to replenish the path every couple of years or so, depending on how much use the path or area gets – it does get kicked about.
- Also blackbirds really like it – they will spread it all over the shop.
- You can also use bark chips as a mulch around plants, but as it breaks down it takes nitrogen from the soil. So either add a nitrogen feed or use bark that's already broken down – composted bark.

GRAVEL GARDENS ...

Sometimes people want a gravel garden like the one Beth Chatto has created near Colchester. It's a great solution to join hard standing areas and planted areas seamlessly together – it's especially good for car parking in front gardens. But the plants in gravel gardens like this aren't planted in gravel. They are planted in the absolute best soil that is possible to put in. The gravel around the plants is just on the surface.

Paving

The choice of paving available is enormous. As is the way with many things, the most often used are well used for a reason. Sandstone is an ideal material for gardens and is probably the most common natural paving in our gardens. The sandstone imported from India is very reasonably priced (although your environmental conscience may have a niggle about this – several suppliers guarantee that their sandstone is ethically sourced). York stone is a sandstone, but from Yorkshire and more expensive than the stuff imported from India. Indian York is the confusing name sometimes used for Indian sandstone.

It's always difficult to choose a stone from a single sample and also to know how it will age. It may be lovely and cream now but in a year's time will it be grey and black? The best way to get a real view of how it will look over a wide area and how it will wear in is to see the paving used in someone's garden. Failing that, many builders' merchants have show gardens outside and it's possible to see how the stone looks over a wider area. But don't just choose the stone, you also need to specify ...

1. Riven or sawn

Riven is split along natural lines and will have an uneven natural-looking surface. Sawn will have dead straight edges and top.

2. Size

The size of the stones – big or small? Smaller will look busier and more detailed. I tend to go for bigger – in a small area they look less fussy and in a big area they will look in proportion.

3. Pattern

The laying pattern can be random or regular.

Verticals
Walls, Fences & Trellis

Once the horizontals – the floors – are sorted, the next things to think about are the verticals – the walls, the fences, the hedges. The verticals I'm talking about aren't just to go around the edge of the garden and mark the boundary. Verticals can be used to divide up the garden and create wonderful new spaces. They set the tone and the proportions of your new garden and generally speaking they are pretty easy to look after, so a great friend of the low maintenance garden.
Verticals have loads of different uses.

Functions	So ...
Mark boundary	If it's just a case of marking a boundary, a low picket fence may be enough and be welcoming as well.
Divide garden	These don't have to be solid and high. They can be low, implied boundaries, or a see-through one of airy plants or trellis work.
Screen eyesores	These need to be tall enough and dense enough to hide the view.
Buffer against noise	Earth bunds are very good at screening from noise. Fences and hedges can help too.
Filter winds	Solid boundaries are less successful than partially open ones. Solid boundaries tend to push the wind up and cause turbulence, rather than slowing and calming the wind.
Make hidden areas	To create hidden areas you need something quite substantial and dense – a hedge, a wall or trellis.
Backdrop for sculpture	Sculptures can be beautifully framed against a flat plane of hedge or wall.

Of these the two main uses are to form a boundary and to make divisions within the garden.

One — Boundaries

Especially in a small garden the boundaries are incredibly important – like the walls of a room. If they are dilapidated and a hotchpotch mixture the whole place will look terrible. A great way to bring the whole garden together is to make the boundaries look the same all the way around.

1. You can do this by planting climbers but these tend to be slow and high maintenance.
2. So a better way is to use trellis or battens to clad the walls.
3. Render and paint the walls to give a really sleek finish.

Or use a combination – but a patterned, regular combination of these.

Regulations ...

Planning regulations tend to be quite strict over boundaries especially where they back onto a public right of way like a road or path. It's always best to check what you're allowed to do – both as far as height and material is concerned and to make sure you don't block lines of sight for cars.

The walls don't have to be completely covered to give a finished look. In this design, by the Garden Trellis Company, light painted trellis has been used along the top of a fence and a wall to give a real unity to the garden without concealing all of the fences and walls.

High old hedges can be loads of hard work and really difficult to maintain. Especially hedges of things like privet which are very fast growers and can need cutting three times a year. I would take them out and replace with a slower grower like yew, or a solid boundary or fence. If you choose yew and if you cut it in August, it should only need a once-a-year cut.

Two — Divides

It's not just around the edges that verticals are important. If you are creating rooms in the garden you need to separate off different areas. These separations don't have to be complete – a low wall will give the impression of a different area without making an imposing statement. Divides can also help to screen unwanted views in the garden and outside. A marine ply wall can hide a staircase or the bins.

Ways to divide up the garden

- Walls
- Trellis
- Plants
- Hedges

Walls

Walls are a favourite for a low-maintenance garden – they can look slick, sleek, modern and architectural – and no gardening in sight.

1. Brick walls are seriously expensive to build but they can look wonderful and a walled or part-walled garden is a lovely addition to the house.

2. It's possible to build walls of concrete block work and render and paint them. These blocks are bigger than bricks and cheaper so it will cost less to build the wall. However it will need maintenance – the paint will probably need touching up every couple of years. Also concrete blocks, being larger, don't do curves very well.

3. However, render is great if you want a flat coloured wall. Bright colours are a really exciting addition to a garden. An even easier way to get the same effect is to build a divide from marine ply and paint it.

4. Capping – this is the layer on top of a wall that stops the rain getting inside it. It seems like a small detail but it can completely transform the character of a wall. If you want your painted, rendered wall to look sleek and modern don't use any capping at all – use beading under the render, this will give the most modern look. The more rustic the capping, the less sleek and the more it will start to look Spanish. If you put roof tiles along the top of the wall, you've gone the whole Mediterranean way.

5. Lights on walls – these plain coloured surfaces are just perfect for shadows. The sun, of course, will create great shadows and lights can shine through foliage to make wonderful shapes after dark.

6. Walls don't just have to create divides – they can hold water features. Modern water features go with rendered walls beautifully. Walls can also hold up in-built seats.

Trellis and battens

Woodwork screens are really coming into their own in design right now and there are some truly beautiful examples of woodwork screens around. There are two main trends.

1. The 'modern' with slick lines or horizontal wood.
2. The more traditional with really beautifully designed and painted close squares of trellis panels. This one is designed by the Garden Trellis Company.

Plants and hedges

Hedges will provide a great, quite low-maintenance barrier, but so will taller shrubs and things like bamboo, even small trees can give an implied boundary with a wonderful repeated line of verticals in their trunks. At the other end of the scale, tall grasses will also give a gauzy, see-through barrier.

RETAINING WALLS ...

Retaining walls hold back earth so that flat areas can be created where previously there may have been a slope. These need to be strong and to have very good drainage behind or weep holes in them so that water does not build up behind them.

Plant design

I know that this book is all about making stunning gardens using design and decoration – treating the outside space exactly as you would treat an inside space – but gardens are different. Generally people expect a garden to have greenery; it's very rare to find a garden without at least some planting and that planting does mean more maintenance. So how do you have greenery without loads of work?

The key is to keep the number of plants down, use the planting only where you need it and choose your plants well. This chapter and the next will help you do that.

Planting

Fewer plants will mean less work, so think about more paved areas, decking and paths. Where you do have plants these are the most low-maintenance options . . .

1. Large architectural plants
2. Shrubs
3. Trees
4. Evergreens
5. Slow growers
6. Drought resistant planting
7. Bulbs
8. Vegetables – I add these to the list, not because they're low maintenance but because you may want to grow some. It is possible to do so without too much hard work . . .

1. Architectural plants

These have strong, bold shapes and can hold an entire area on their own. Buy one of these large and it will be expensive, but probably not as expensive as tens of little plants to fill the same space and, most importantly, the one large plant will be a lot easier to look after.

2. Shrubs

These do have a dated reputation about them, but they can be very 21st century if you only use one type of shrub and plant it en masse to make a bold statement. Or try choosing just two or three types and planting them in waving lines, with a taller shrub behind and a lower one in front.

TIP
Whatever you're planting – the fewer different types of plant you use, the lower the maintenance. This is what supermarkets and car parks learnt a long time ago – but don't let that put you off!

3. Trees

Trees are pretty much a no-maintenance plant; even in a small garden trees can be used to give height – in fact a smaller garden is perfect for a tree – it doesn't take up much space on the ground but is great value for shade and interest. They may get too big after a few years, but you can take them out or trim them. Some trees are better than others.

Five of the best trees | Why?

Five of the best trees	Why?
Autumn flowering cherry	All the benefits of a cherry tree, plus it flowers in milder spells all through the winter.
Judas tree	The purple-leaved one is especially beautiful. This is slow growing and has the most delicious pink flowers against heart-shaped purple leaves.
Witch hazel	Great scented flowers in late winter and lovely autumn-coloured leaves.
Coral bark maple	Incredible autumn colour and bright red stems through the winter.
Silver birch	These have beautiful smooth white stems and delicate leaves that catch the breeze. The multi-stemmed ones are particularly nice.

4. Evergreens

If I say evergreen shrub you probably think of something even granny would think was dated. But they give great value for pretty much no input and if I say 'bamboo', no one could call that dated. Bamboos are, I think, the perfect evergreen plant for a small garden and you couldn't get much more contemporary. They don't have a large footprint on the ground, they are evergreen, they are stylish and they are incredibly low maintenance.

5. Slow growers

The other things to look for are plants which don't shoot away too much. Slow growers will not need pruning or chopping back twice a year, they'll take their time to fill out but all of that is just putting off the fateful day when you have to do some gardening.

6. Drought-resistant planting

If your bugbear is having to water things you can either put in an automatic watering system or you can put in things which can withstand drought. Try grasses, grey-leaved plants (the grey leaves are a mechanism to prevent water loss) and Mediterranean plants, like lavenders, olive trees and rosemary.

TIP

If you do put in lots of different types of plants at least make sure they have the same sort of requirements. So, for example, put drought-resistant plants together.

7. Bulbs

Most bulbs are wonderfully low maintenance – once you get them in! They pop their heads up, flower and fade away again without a murmur – just perfect for a low-maintenance garden.

1. Choose ones which will come up year after year and don't have to be lifted.
2. It's great to have lots of the same sort of bulb rather than just one or two. These will be a job to put in but should be a stunning display every year after that.

Bulbs to avoid

Avoid those that have to be lifted each year like tulips and hyacinths. Also I'd avoid daffodils. With daffodils you're meant to leave the old leaves for six weeks or so after the flowers have died. The leaves look awful. Much better to go for something that comes and goes quietly.

Planting

Planting bulbs, especially lots of them, can quite literally be a pain, but once it's done, it's done.

Unless, that is, you have squirrels. When I worked in the gardens of a grand country house, one year we planted over a thousand beautiful scillas under the

1. Keep the patch small.
2. Have it next to the house – so you can see it from the kitchen window and don't forget about them.
3. Ensure they are in the sun.
4. The answer may be to grow vegetables in containers. The pots need to be quite deep and large but it's a great way to keep the maintenance down.
5. Just grow one or two things the first year – if you like them you can always do more next year.
6. Buy little plants from the garden centre (called 'plugs') and grow them on rather than trying to grow from seed. It's just as rewarding and much less effort. Lettuces, strawberries, courgettes can all be grown from plugs.

trees. The next year about six came up. If you think this might happen in your garden, bed in some chicken wire over the ground after you've planted the bulbs to keep the thieves out.

How to plant

Usually the instructions specific to the bulb are on the packet. Most bulbs should be planted at twice their own depth and with the pointed bit upwards.

8. Vegetables

If you want a really low-maintenance garden you wouldn't have vegetables at all. But life's not always logical.

Sometimes it's nice to have a small area, an area you can cope with, that you can look at every day, a patch to grow stuff. If you do want to grow vegetables or herbs try to …

Herb garden

1. Keep it small and, like the vegetables, near the house.
2. Containers are ideal for herbs; if you can get something with different compartments it would be ideal to keep the different herbs apart.
3. Just grow herbs you like to use – so you take little bits off regularly – which is just the way to keep them looking good.
4. Buy little plants from garden centres to start off, growing from seed will be time-consuming and probably fruitless.

Weeding or chemicals

Most people want to be as organic as possible and not use chemicals. However, they can be very useful and a lot easier than trying to weed. My problem with them is that once I've sprayed I forget to tidy up in the days afterwards and instead of looking at lovely healthy weeds I'm then looking at sick and dying ones.

There are some rules about weedkillers

1. Use as a last resort.
2. Always read the label.
3. Use as little as possible.
4. Make sure children and pets aren't around and try to spray early in the morning so you don't spray bees.

Types of weedkiller

1. **Contact weedkiller**   kills exactly what it comes into contact with and no more.

2. **Systemic weedkiller**   glyphosate is the most common – this moves through the plant to kill the roots as well.

3. **Residual weedkiller**   stays in the soil and will prevent anything growing for months or years. You would normally use this on paths – somewhere you will never want to grow anything.

The most common kinds you will see are systemic. These claim to be deactivated on contact with the soil but I still keep my children off for a while, just in case. They enter the plants they kill through their leaves – so technically you can spray all around the base of taller trees and shrubs and kill all the weeds at ground level without harming the tall thing, as long as you avoid its leaves.

Watering

This can be really time-consuming and if there's a hosepipe ban on, almost unbearably, back-breakingly so. Two main solutions – get the water to the plants another way, or make sure the plants don't need so much water.

1. Leaky hose systems are great. They really are just hosepipes that go from the tap. When they get to the flower bed or container, you put in a connector and swap for a hose made of material which allows the water to seep out. You can either turn the tap on and off yourself or have a timer to do it for you.

2. Mulches and coverings can help to keep moisture in and keep the weeds down. Things like bark or a water-permeable membrane around the base of plants are OK but they look a bit naff. If you're going to put something on the soil make it something that really does some good – use something which improves the soil. Well-rotted manure is a magic substance; it will help to stop the soil getting waterlogged in winter and help it hold on to water in the summer.

3. Choose plants that are drought resistant.

Slash and burn

There have been quite a few times when I've been in a garden which has been completely overgrown – I mean completely awash with stuff. The owners, unsure of pruning techniques and scared of killing the plants, had been frozen into inaction. There are two reasons to prune, one is for your benefit and one is for the plant's. Since I think people are more important than plants I'd always make sure there's plenty of room in the garden for the people – cut it back, take it away, it's your garden!

A special word about roses

I don't like roses and if you want a trouble-free, low-maintenance garden you would not let a rose cross the threshold. However, I know people like them and will put up with their evil thorns, their diseases and their lack of any interest whatsoever in winter – but they definitely aren't low-maintenance plants

WHAT'S A HIGH-MAINTENANCE PLANT?

It's interesting to see what makes plants high maintenance, just to make them easy to avoid.

1. Tender ones which need to be brought in over winter.
2. Ones susceptible to disease that have to be sprayed.
3. Flowering plants that have to be deadheaded or look terrible.
4. Thirsty plants that need to be watered every day.
5. Rampant growers that need to be cut back several times a year to keep out of the way and looking good.
6. Plants that need to be staked.
7. Plants that only live for a year or two and have to be replaced.

Containers

What do people like doing in their garden? Sitting, lying, eating, sleeping, reading, yes yes, but they also, often, like tending their containers. Even the person who really doesn't like gardening, who thinks it's a waste of time, will not mind a few containers. Why is this?

It's certainly, on the face of it, illogical. Containers are, inch for inch, incredibly high maintenance. They need planting up and deadheading, watering and feeding. All the things I'll spend the rest of the book telling you how to avoid. So why do people like them? The answer is very instructive.

- Because they're small enough to keep on top of.
- Because they're small enough to look after in a few minutes.
- But you do still get the feeling you're gardening, there's a sense of achievement when something you've put in starts to grow.
- Also, very importantly, container gardening involves a fair amount of shopping. Buying plants and pots is fun.

TIPS FOR CONTAINERS

- Larger will need less watering.
- Make sure the soil or compost doesn't go right to the top of the container, so there's room for you to put the water in.
- Install an automatic watering system.
- Group them together rather than dot them about so you don't have to traipse about to look after them.
- Use water-retaining granules. You buy these from the garden centre and mix them with the compost when you plant the containers up.
- Choose plants that can tolerate some neglect. Geraniums are great – if you forget to water these for a few days they will probably be fine.
- Use slow-release feed pellets – put these in when you plant up the container and there'll be enough food in there for the season.

Plants for containers

You don't have to do bedding – you can use perennials, bulbs, grasses, even trees if your containers are big enough. If you choose something which can cope with a lack of water from time to time, it will be happier.

Which plants?

This is the low-maintenance guide to low-maintenance plants. Rather than reel off loads to choose from, I've put some different categories below and in each category I've selected five of the best plants. Where those plants are meant to go together in a scheme, I've made sure they'll combine nicely and put the largest ones first in the list (they'll go at the back). So you can take any of these lists and (depending on the size of your garden) buy threes or fives or tens of each of the plants to make a stunning low-maintenance garden.

Lowest of the low

These are the plants you can just put in and leave; at most all they'll need is a once-a-year trim.

1. **Mexican orange blossom** – Evergreen with white flowers in summer.
2. **Oregon grape** – Evergreen with yellow scented flowers in winter.
3. **Box** – It's great to make shapes out of this evergreen - the play dough of the garden.
4. **Black lily turf** – It looks like black grass and will slowly spread to cover an area.
5. **Bugle** – Beautiful purple flowers in summer on a spreading evergreen ground-cover plant.

Winter interest

If you really want to make sure your garden looks good in winter try these.

1. **Mexican orange blossom** – Evergreen with white flowers in summer.
2. **Dogwood** – The stems of these plants come in brilliant reds, purples and yellows which make a great display in winter.
3. **Daphne** – Early flowering with delicate pink flowers.
4. **Bugle** – Evergreen spreading plant that will cover the ground with shiny dark leaves.
5. **Snowdrops** – White flowers in January and February.

Low–maintenance arrangement that changes through the seasons

If you want things coming and going at different times of the year.

1. **Tussock grass** – This tall grass will come up through summer and its bronze seedheads will stay well into winter.
2. **Japanese anemones** – Tall flowers from August through to end of September.
3. **Elephant's ears** – These are evergreen and flower in the depths of winter.
4. **Lily turf** – Evergreen grass-like plant which flowers in autumn.
5. **Snowdrops** – These fill the gap between the dead of winter and spring.

Architectural plants for instant impact

6

You probably don't need to choose more than one plant from this list to make a statement in the garden, especially if you buy it big.

1. New Zealand flax – A bold clump of strappy leaves. The purple ones look great against a light background.

2. Century plant – This spiky plant is not very hardy so only try it if you have a sheltered spot, but it makes a striking statement in a modern setting.

3. Pittosporum – Evergreen with interesting shapes to its leaves and scented flowers.

4. Stag's horn sumach – This has great autumn colour and a sculptural shape in winter, just right for a single, centrepiece plant.

5. Cabbage palm – Spiky leaves from a central point make this look like an explosion of colour in a light setting.

Using one type of plant over a large area

A great way to keep the maintenance down and to look stylish is to use 10, 20 or more of just one type of plant.

1. Lavender – You do need to trim this once a year but it has many benefits.

2. Dogwood – These look like nice enough shrubs in summer, but in winter they have crazy coloured stems.

3. Pheasant's tail grass – Evergreen with coppery foliage in autumn and through winter.

4. Golden male fern – An evergreen for a shady spot, it grows to about half a metre.

5. Rock rose – Shrubby evergreen with rose-like flowers in summer.

Drought-resistant plants

If your soil is poor or watering is your least favourite job, try these.

1. Butterfly bush – The one called 'Black Knight' has dark flowers in summer which smell divine.

2. Bear's breeches – Tall stately plant with purple and white spikes of summer flowers.

3. Yarrow – These come in shades of yellows and reds and flower in late summer.

4. Lady's mantle – Yellow flowers above soft green leaves.

5. Bugle – Evergreen ground cover with purple flowers in early summer.

The most useful plants ...

Some of the plants appear more than once on these lists – these are the real winners in a low-maintenance garden. One tall, one medium and one ground cover – Mexican orange blossom, Dogwood and Bugle are the winners!

Climbers

If you want really low maintenance you won't put in climbers at all. Try using things like bamboos or shrubs to cover a wall. Climbers need tying in and cutting back or if they are self-clinging they will grow where you don't want them and you'll have to battle to keep them in place, but if you really want to have them these ones will reward a little work.

1. Armand clematis – Evergreen with scented white flowers in spring.

2. Star jasmine – Evergreen with scented white flowers in summer.

3. Climbing hydrangea – Good for a shady wall and has seedheads which look great even after the flowers have gone.

4. Golden hop – It dies right down to the ground each year but makes a spectacular show through the summer.

5. Honeysuckle – Scented flowers through the summer and some varieties are evergreen.

Plants for containers

Really, you can put anything into a container, but for low maintenance you need something that doesn't need deadheading, doesn't need watering too often and looks good throughout the year so you don't need to dig it up and replace it.

1. Sedums – The archetypal low-maintenance container plant – even if you go away for two weeks in high summer, once you water it again it will (probably!) come back to life.

2. Box – They just stick around doing their thing, although they don't appreciate being left without water so a leaky hose in the back of the container would be good.

3. Ivy – One of the best container displays I ever saw was a huge long line of containers on the side of a building with ivy hanging from them.

4. Christmas box – A great plant for containers, evergreen with scented flowers in winter.

5. Black lily turf – This dark-leaved plant looks wonderful in a small zinc or silver-coloured container.

Bulbs

Bulbs do take effort to put in, but after that these ones will look after themselves. The general rule is to plant them two seasons before they flower – so if, for example, you're reading this in spring, think about putting in some autumn-flowering crocuses or nerines.

Winter
Winter aconite
Snowdrops
Spring
Windflower
Fritillary
Summer
Ornamental onions – Allium
Gladioli
Autumn
Crocus
Nerine

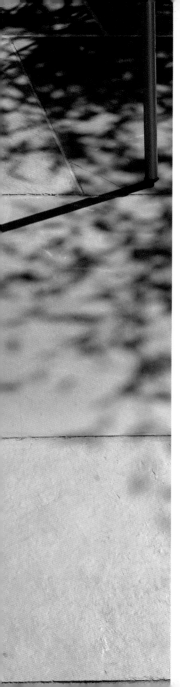

Lighting

If you want a garden to look magnificent, fun and exciting with no maintenance – try garden lighting.

Things are moving so quickly now in lighting: that which was really avant-garde just a few years ago is now in every DIY shop.

There are two types of lighting in the garden, sunlight and artificial light. It's easy to forget that sunlight is a wonderful light source. Think about shadows of trees on grass, of reflections in water, of plants against a crisp wall.

Natural light

The thing about natural light is that it changes through the day and through the year. It's worth, if you have the time, thinking about how it changes and how to make the most of it. I was in my friend's garden last week late in the evening and the sun was just going down – wouldn't it be wonderful to have some shimmering grasses and a tall, purple-leaved smoke bush to catch that golden hour of sunlight? No, she said, I need that space for my washing line. Some people are romantic and some people not.

Making a dark area as bright as possible …

If you have a really dark enclosed area in the garden there are several things you can do to make the most of whatever light it does get.

1. **Reflective surfaces** – Mirrors, silver containers, even a water feature will all reflect light about.
2. **Paint the walls** – Render them first – the smoother and lighter the surface the more the light will bounce off it. So a wall which has been rendered and painted a white colour will give back aeons more light than a light-sucking red brick wall.
3. **Put light-reflective elements on the ground** – Light-coloured gravels will help to bounce light up. The best surface to make the most of every drop of light, is a smooth light-coloured tile or white limestone.
4. **Plants** – Don't put in any heavy dark green plants on walls, instead, keep them to a minimum and only have variegated or light green plants.
5. **Put in artificial lights** – You can help the daylight along a little with spots and uplighters.

Artificial lights

Two types
In the realm of artificial lights there are two types of these as well, one functional, for safety, and the other for show.

Functional
If there are any steps, paths, ponds or access ways these will need to be lit so people don't trip. There are also motion sensor lights to help burglars see their way about. Traditionally this has been what garden lighting has been about.

Decorative
Beyond this functional role, garden lighting has a huge part to play in making gardens exciting and fun. I know people say that evenings are rarely warm enough to sit out and enjoy those lights – but think of the view you get from the sitting room window, lighting can make a magical scene.

Buying lights
Lighting is now big business on the Internet, everything from cheap and cheerful spots and fairy lights to serious bits of art. I've put some addresses below that I've found helpful in the past.

Lighting designer
If you're serious about lighting, do think about getting a lighting designer in – they can give some wonderful ideas which will lift even a modest garden into the realms of art.

Lighting effects

Mirroring

Underwater lighting

Floodlighting

Uplighting

Grazing

Spotlighting

Backlighting

Ten ideas

1. Put the lighting on different circuits so you can light different areas of the garden.

2. If you're re-doing the garden put in ducting even if you don't want to put in lighting – it means you can add the lighting cables easily later.

3. Always catch the light you create – don't just point a light in the air; it needs to be lighting something.

4. If you have a flat surface like a wall, think about creating shadows on it.

5. Mood lighting is available now which changes colour if you want it to.

6. Have the switches indoors so the lighting is easy to put on.

7. Try to make sure any lights don't annoy the neighbours.

8. The main view you are likely to see of the lighting is from inside the house (however much we may dream of long evenings supping wine outside it really doesn't happen much) and this is the view you will see throughout the year. So the lighting has to look good from this viewpoint and in winter as well as summer.

9. Most of the time you won't see the light fitting – so you don't need to spend an arm and leg on it. As long as it's robust enough to withstand the weather over the years.

10. If in doubt you can't beat candles for a romantic look.

Electricity

Most garden lighting is powered by low-voltage electricity. A transformer steps the main voltage down to 12 volts before it goes out to the garden. It's easy enough to do, it just requires a transformer plugged into a socket, but always get a qualified electrician in to lay electric cable, sockets etc.

No wires

Solar lighting is getting more exciting and more affordable. These are great for a quick fix and just for fun.

Water

Here's another one of those things that shouldn't enter into your head if you want a really low-maintenance garden, but if you like water and enjoy mucking about with a pond it won't be work, it's fun. If you want water but as little work as possible, go for an off-the-peg, contained water feature.

Do you really want a water feature?

To decide if you want a water feature and what kind of feature you want here are some questions …

Do you want moving water?

You will need a pump to lift the water and therefore an electricity supply. How it falls will determine the sound you get – a trickle or a gush?

TIP

To make the most of the sound make sure the feature is near the house or a sitting area.

Do you want reflections and still water?

That indicates you probably want a pond rather than an off-the-peg feature.

Do you want fish?

You definitely want a pond and if you want fish it needs to be at least two feet deep, and deeper still for specialised fish like Koi.

Pond

If you do want a pond and want to keep the maintenance down, the bigger the better strangely enough: it can keep its temperature more easily and it acts as a more stable habitat.

Pond – keeping it low maintenance

1. Do it properly in the first place – use a really good lining so, hopefully, you won't get holes in it.
2. Have a really solid edging to the pond – paving stones are good for most of the edge and keep the lining well hidden; but maybe also have a little pebble 'beach' for frogs at some point.
3. Don't put really strong growing plants like bulrush in or you'll be forever trying to get rid of them.

Plants to avoid

Avoid these, not just because they'll overwhelm your pond, but also because they are escaping into the wild in the UK and damaging native species.

- Water fern
- Floating pennywort
- Parrot's feather
- Australian swamp stonecrop
- Curly waterweed
- Water primrose.

Water features

- These are available from garden centres and online, in every kind of look from Italian Renaissance to steel.
- The water is recycled with a pump and there is often no standing water so it's safer for children to be around.
- As long as there are no animals, fish or plants in the feature you can use chemicals to keep the water clear.

Stating the obvious ...

It sounds obvious once you know, but it's worth saying. Pretty much all water features have a contained water system, so apart from topping them up occasionally you don't need a water supply. If they have a pump you will need a power supply though.

Lighting

Lighting water features adds to their use – especially if they can be seen from the house. If you're lighting a pond make sure the light doesn't skim the top of the water – this will just show up all the debris.

Siting a water feature

- Put it somewhere you can enjoy it and see it either from the house or from a sitting area.

- The plants in the pond need sunlight so if possible put the pond in a sunny spot.

- A 'natural' pond will look a lot more natural if it's placed at the lowest point of a garden, where water would gather naturally. If there is no lower point you might want to think about sinking the pond and making banks around it – but more soil will have to be brought out and this will add to the cost.

- Whether a pond or a feature, it will look best if it's 'designed in' to the garden and not just plonked on top. So a specific place is made for the feature.

- The best bet for a pond or feature is to surround it with plants – even if it means having a path through to get to the water.

- A water feature as a focal point needs to be substantial enough to hold the area, if you find yourself with something that's too small, put it to the side in the beds where it doesn't have to work so hard.

If you don't want any of the work involved with water, it might be better to have a statue or a sculpture instead.

Decoration

Sculpture and art are great friends of the low-maintenance garden – they look great, involve shopping and are pretty much no maintenance.

It's a very personal thing – what you think will look nice in your garden is entirely your decision, but whatever the specific thing is there are some tips to help you get its position right.

Ten tips for placing sculpture

1. Sculpture gives personality and character to a garden – it can change the whole atmosphere of the place.

2. Where you place an ornament is incredibly important. Put two urns on either side of a path and you're inviting thoughts of grandeur. Put the same urns on their side in the long grass and we've moved to an entirely more romantic place.

3. It is very difficult to get a piece to work as the centre of a garden or area, the scale, the feel and the setting have to be exactly right – it's a work of art in itself to site a centrepiece sculpture well. It's safer to place the sculpture to the side, as something to come across, rather than centre stage.

4. Visit sculpture parks to see what can work in the open and how it's displayed.

5. If you are making it a centrepiece you can either choose the sculpture to fit your garden or change your garden to fit the sculpture.

6. Light the art or sculpture so you can enjoy it after dark as well.

7. If it really is special, think about putting in a seat nearby from where you can look at it.

8. Don't put more than one piece of sculpture on display at once or it will look like a sculpture gallery. If you have more than one piece use hedges, walls or plants to try to make it so that only one is visible at a time.

9. You may still get it wrong, even people who have been doing this for years make mistakes and need to rearrange things several times before it looks right.

10. Look out for open studios in your area or student shows for something unique for your garden.

Wildlife

No beating about the bush this is a great excuse to have a messy, unkempt garden. Wildlife, on the whole, doesn't like neat. A well-kept lawn is a wildlife desert; a pruned, preened, sprayed and tidied flower bed is never going to be buzzing with life. Making an oasis for wildlife is a different way of designing gardens. Yes, still create rooms, but what you're trying to do is to recreate habitats and food chains. Attract bugs and you'll attract birds. Attract bees and your plants will be pollinated and you'll have fruit for other wildlife. A garden that has some of this thought put into it is an exciting place to be, it gives another dimension to gardens and they hum with life.

Gardens matter ...

In the UK there are 15 million gardens. Two million acres of land in this country is garden. Every garden can help to keep bees and butterflies alive when outside the garden supportive habitats are increasingly scarce.

Benefits of a wildlife garden
- Attracts birds, bees and butterflies
- Saves time – you really need it to be less tidy
- Good for children – they can lose themselves in the undergrowth and find hedgehogs, newts and worms.

Tips to make a wildlife-friendly garden

1. Try to mimic the way the land would be naturally if your garden wasn't on it. For most of the UK there would be layers of different plants – a tree layer, a hedgerow layer, a shrubby layer and the undergrowth. Each of these would have its own wildlife population.

2. Keep the plants that local wildlife can use, that means natives or near natives.

3. A pond is the single best thing to encourage wildlife. The water will attract amphibians, bugs, birds and more.

4. Use rainwater to top the pond up, so the chemical balance remains correct.

5. Don't use chemicals in the garden.

6. Keep the paths neat to make sure the whole thing doesn't look overrun.

7. Don't cut down dead flowers, their seedheads may be food for birds.

8. Don't burn dead wood make a stick fence. You lay any sticks you find in the garden on the ground in a neat row. To help keep them from falling about put some of the more sturdy ones in vertically and push them into the earth. As it builds up it will make a fence but, and this is the clever bit, it will never overflow. The bottom sticks rot down as you fill it up from the top and, in the meantime it's a home for all sorts of bugs, beetles and bees.

9. Nettles and ivy are wonderful for wildlife; if you can bear it leave them alone.

Lawn or wildflower meadow?

A great way to keep the work down is to mow only part of the lawn and let the rest grow up and form a meadow. Now traditionally this wildflower meadow should be cut in July and then treated as lawn after that until spring – always taking the cuttings off, but I've found it's perfectly acceptable to leave the cut until September. You get a couple of months more with the lovely long grass, and if you cut it late it will look awful for a couple of weeks but the grass is growing so strongly in the autumn it will soon recover. If you're very clever, or lucky, you will only have to cut it once a year. If the soil is too rich you'll get docks and nettles growing – best to remove them by hand and, hopefully, as the soil gets worse, they should stop coming back.

Native plants

To find out what plants are specifically native to your area go to the postcode plant database at the Natural History Museum www.nhm.ac.uk/nature-online/ life/plants-fungi/postcode-plants. You put in your postcode and it'll tell you what's native.

Here are five shrubs that are widely native to the UK

Alder
Buckthorn
Dog rose
Guelder rose
Hawthorn

Bees

Most bees won't sting you and they are incredibly important to the environment and to farming, as well as for pollinating fruit trees and bushes. So if your lavender or Californian lilac is humming with noise on a summer's day, don't be scared, they're not wasps, they're bees doing a vital job and they really won't bother you if you leave them be.

Flowering plants to attract bees

Butterfly bush
Catmint
Lavenders
Wild marjoram
Perennial sunflowers

Inspiration

It's one thing knowing *how* to do something, it's quite another knowing *what* to do. The best garden designers are always aware of what other people are doing and what previous designers have done. It is truly helpful to look at other designs and see what you can use in your own garden.

So here are 10 gardens which are all very different but they are designed to be low maintenance. To make the gardens as useful as possible, I've put plans along with lots of captioned pictures, explaining the design and how it came about.

Built-in seating

This is a great example of the garden as an outside room. The owners wanted a sitting area in the garden and a room that was easy to maintain with no more than a brush down.

There are plants but they have been added discreetly and to enhance the lines of the design. By keeping to a very limited range of plants and making sure they are all evergreen, Stuart Craine, the designer, has kept the maintenance to a minimum. So rather than have to pick through the borders and decide what to do with each plant every few weeks, these are plants which require a once-, or at worst twice-a-year trim back and no more. Kept in raised beds they really are the outside equivalent of house plants. Many of the plants are also herbs so the garden will be beautifully scented throughout the year.

But to stop the scene becoming too monotonous and to mark the seasons, bulbs have been put in. By using only one type of bulb (alliums), these visitors are easier to look after and add to the design rather than detract from it.

The design itself uses wonderfully strong and simple horizontal and vertical lines. As you look at the garden from the house, the vertical lines of the fences and low hedges vanish off into the distance, but they are countered by strong horizontals provided by the lines of planting and raised beds. The whole is a carefully balanced composition.

Garden Plan

Pleached magnolia (pleached trees have been trained to give a 'hedge on stilts') at the rear of the garden provide screening without interfering with the view of the wall.

This garden uses a limited palette of plants, planted en masse to keep the maintenance down. Using evergreens also helps to reduce maintenance and means the garden will look good in winter and summer.

Built-in seats form the space within the garden and mean there is year-round seating without having to drag chairs in and out or store them.

Stuart has created spaces within the garden – but he has done this with low divisions so you can see right down the garden.

All of the boundaries of the garden have been unified by having the same woodwork around the top bringing the heights to the same level.

The back wall has been rendered and painted to match the raised beds along the side of the garden.

Using clipped box to carry on the line of the built-in seat gives a quirky detail.

The garden is quite long and thin, so to make sense of the space Stuart has created an implied room halfway down the garden which makes a great place to sit and to entertain, and widens out the garden.

Grey/black slate tiles on the ground, laid formally in a stretcher bond pattern, give a modern look to the garden.

▶ The wall on this side has been left exposed so the beautiful old bricks can be seen. The three lines of materials – a low box hedge, wall and wood trellis above, give strong horizontal lines going off to the bottom of the garden.

▲ It's probably not as important now as it once was, but 'the washing-up view' used to be the main way you would see the garden and the main opportunity to stare out and dream. Dishwashers have lessened its importance, but it's still a major viewing point.

▶ Lines of planting give a strong design element, and also help to keep the maintenance down. Rosemary, purple sage and thyme will waft scents into the enclosed space throughout the year.

▼ Beautiful hardwood screens have been custom-made for this garden.

◀ The simplicity is continued against the house. Two bay trees, trained into lollipop shapes, stand at either side of the back doors.

I

Walled

How to get a walled garden that's easy to look after? A traditional walled garden is brimming with plants and flowers – and with work – but if you don't have all of those plants the walls will dominate the space they enclose. The owners of this garden brought in designer Mary Bullock to try and work out how to square this circle.

Before

How to introduce interest but keep down the maintenance? Mary has solved those design problems beautifully and what she's created is a stylish, low-maintenance garden. Overall she's used strong straight lines to divide the area, lines which are given by the straightness of the surrounding walls – curves just wouldn't look right in this area. To create different spaces, rather than use upright divides, she's made implied divisions and created changes in level to give different rooms and to make sense of the individual areas. Not only do these levels help to define areas, they also add interest to the open square of land that the garden was.

The implied divisions use low hedges, planted beds and paving to separate off different areas.

Raising the seating area in the corner is a clever way to add interest and create a room within the garden, but even better, Mary has used the height to make an interesting water feature. The water falls down in three stages, running along the step from one pool to another.

Overall Mary has created a stylish garden which doesn't rely on plants for its interest; instead it relies on good design and a wonderful water feature.

2

Garden Plan

A raised sitting area in the corner creates a room within a room in the garden.

Planting along the rear walls helps to break up the brickwork without covering it.

The water feature is in two sections – a raised pool to the right and a ground-level pool to the left. Water falls between the two as it flows across the entrance to the raised sitting area.

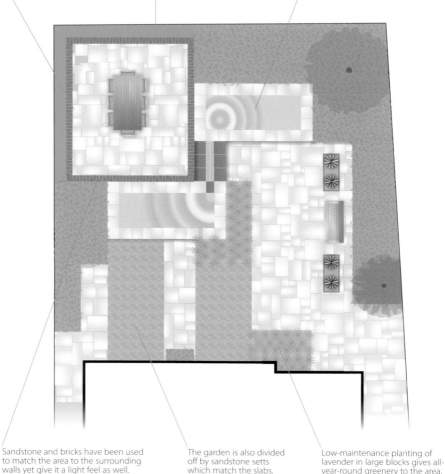

Sandstone and bricks have been used to match the area to the surrounding walls yet give it a light feel as well.

The garden is also divided off by sandstone setts which match the slabs.

Low-maintenance planting of lavender in large blocks gives all-year-round greenery to the area.

▶ Sandstone setts have been interspersed with slabs of the same material to give interesting patterns to the flooring and help to divide the garden.

▲ The elegant shapes of the pools and sitting areas can be clearly seen from the first floor of the house. This is a view that is hugely important in most gardens – it's worth thinking about what you will see from up here.

▼ There are some higher-maintenance plants in the garden but they are confined to the perimeter of the space.

▼ The materials of the garden work together beautifully. Red handmade bricks from York Handmade Bricks and Indian sandstone, Fossil Mint.

▶ The rill as it crosses the pathway makes three steps downwards.

▲ The lining is completely built inside the walls of the pools so it is totally out of sight and it is protected from damage.

▼ In the lower pool the planting is kept to one end by an underwater barrier.

▶ Rusted iron obelisks from Room In The Garden help to give height to the garden away from the walls.

Interlocking shapes

This is a very interesting way of tackling quite a common problem. It was a small garden with a step up very near the house. The garden appeared to be falling into the house and gave an uncomfortable subterranean feel to the garden room.

Before

The other problems were the surrounding walls which dominated the space, and a complete lack of definition to the garden.

Amir Schlezinger of MyLandscapes has tackled all three of these issues with a wonderful, bold design. He has pushed that step up right back into the garden. But in doing that he was faced with a problem – push it right back and one space (the higher or the lower) will start to dominate the garden. His ingenious solution is to use 45-degree angles to create two interlocking spaces.

To define the two areas, Amir has used different materials on the floor. At the lower level, leading out from the garden room and at the same level, are decking boards. At the higher level are squares of sandstone. A low box hedge just gives that extra definition and separation to the two spaces.

The dominance of the surrounding walls has been reduced by using a raised bed, filled with tall low-maintenance plants, along the rear and one side of the garden. A built-in bench helps to break up the expanse of rendered and painted wall with a bold, sleek line.

This is a deceptively simple solution which does everything a great garden design should. Amir has taken unprepossessing space and transformed it into a beautiful outdoor room.

Garden Plan

Only six different types of plants have been used – two types of bamboo, Japanese maple, box, New Zealand flax and a Judas tree. This simplicity reinforces the clean lines of the design and makes maintenance easy.

There is plenty of greenery in this garden but by using large specimens and keeping the plants in raised beds the maintenance has been kept low.

At the higher level, sandstone rectangles give a light, modern look.

The surrounding walls with trellis above haven't been changed. Instead, along the rear of the garden a raised bed has been created to allow the eye to look at sleek lines and greenery rather than a tall wall.

The red-leafed maple gives a Japanese feel to the garden in summer and casts pretty shadows on the ground. Along the rear are bamboos – perfect for tall, all-year-round, low-maintenance greenery.

The garden here is on two levels. The change in level could have been made with a straight line across the garden but Amir has created an interesting shape which kicks out at 45 degrees.

To help reinforce the idea of the two different rooms, a low box hedge has been used to enclose the upper area.

At the lower level, hardwood decking makes a wonderful contrast to the stonework around it. It has been laid across the space so the lines help to widen it out.

▶ The same 45-degree angle is used to finish off the raised bed as it approaches the side wall.

▲ At the front of the property, two lollipopped bay trees on either side of the door match a low line of lavenders in the same grey containers.

▲ The risers as well as the treads of this garden have been formed by York stone; this is a good option if the level change isn't great.

▲ The planting scheme relies on large specimens of low-maintenance plants – these fill up the borders with minimal effort.

◀ Previously the level change happened right next to the house. Amir has pushed that level change back into the garden and made a wide usable space right outside the house, continuing at the same level as the inside room, so one large area is created crossing the boundary between inside and out.

▼ Above the garden, a tiny terrace has been redesigned by Amir with matching decking and a simple flower arrangement in the corner.

▲ A built-in seat follows the angle of the raised bed, cutting down further the influence of the vertical plane at the rear of the garden. The seat is cantilevered, built in to the wall behind it, so it appears to be floating. This helps to make the garden look larger – there's nothing to stop the line of the floor, there's also great potential to light below the bench for dramatic effect.

▼ Polished black pebbles – great for keeping weeds down and hiding bare soil; they look really good whether in a bed or in a container.

▶ The raised beds are interesting – they haven't been filled with soil or compost, the plants are in soil at ground level. So the bases of the plants (rarely their best bits) aren't seen and at night uplighting can pick up on all the foliage.

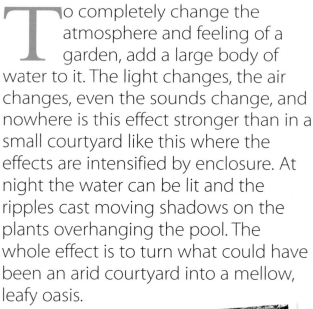

Water

To completely change the atmosphere and feeling of a garden, add a large body of water to it. The light changes, the air changes, even the sounds change, and nowhere is this effect stronger than in a small courtyard like this where the effects are intensified by enclosure. At night the water can be lit and the ripples cast moving shadows on the plants overhanging the pool. The whole effect is to turn what could have been an arid courtyard into a mellow, leafy oasis.

Before

The owners here were very keen on fish and wanted a modern pool to house them. In this garden nearly half the ground space is taken up by a pool.

Pools do take maintenance but larger pools are not really more work than smaller ones, and the pool here is big. To make sure the proportions worked with the rest of the garden the owners brought in Jano Williams, the garden designer, to plan out how it should all work together.

At the other side of the courtyard is an open seating area where there is room for a table and chairs as well as a built-in seat. All around the enclosed space are raised beds full of large specimen architectural plants like bamboos and bananas. These help to give a lush green feel to the area but, safely enclosed in raised beds and kept to the edges of the garden, they don't raise any real maintenance issues.

Garden Plan

Creating a large area of water like this brings a magical quality to the garden, instead of being a harsh, hard courtyard it reflects light and creates movement all through the year.

A few large, low-maintenance plants around the edges of the garden provide enough greenery without making a lot of work.

All the walls have been rendered and painted cream to give a clean, light feel to the space.

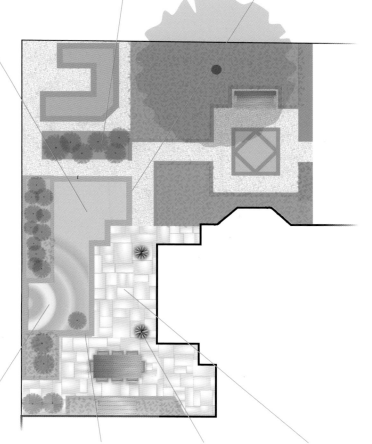

The pool fits into the corner of the garden, but rather than being an L-shape to fit right into the corner it juts out to give a larger area of open water.

The pool is raised to just the right height to sit on the edge and look into the water.

Where extra greenery is needed the clients have added containers with large olive trees.

The main area is divided between hard landscaping and a raised pool – there's no grass and not many plants.

▶ Light-coloured walls, painted with Johnstone's Ivory paint, are perfect to catch the shadows formed by the bamboo.

4

▲ Containers are a great way to break up the paving and mark the entrance to the house. Compared to planted beds these olive trees are much lower maintenance.

▼ This tree fern looks just right here. In a mild winter its leaves will stay on and look good right through to spring. If, however, you live in an exposed area it's best to fold the dying leaves over the crown of the plant to protect the growing area from frosts.

▶ By taking away the grass and confining the plants to the sides there's plenty of room in this courtyard for a large table and chairs.

▲ Raising the pond above ground level makes it look more contemporary and more useful to the design of the patio – it encloses the area and provides seating.

▼ Water lilies thrive in a sheltered environment, this with virtually still water. They are incredibly useful to provide shade for the fish and to help keep algae away from the pond.

▲ From inside the house the design makes a lot of sense. Right outside the sitting room is the largest area of water and its surrounding greenery – a wonderfully lush view.

▼ The paving, used also as capping for the wall, is Indian limestone. It is Marshalls' Silver Birch; it was important to the owners that Marshalls has an ethical policy that ensures fair wages and conditions and doesn't employ child labour.

▶ There's a water feature set into the side wall where water falls over slate. It doesn't disturb the water too much though or the water lilies would not be happy.

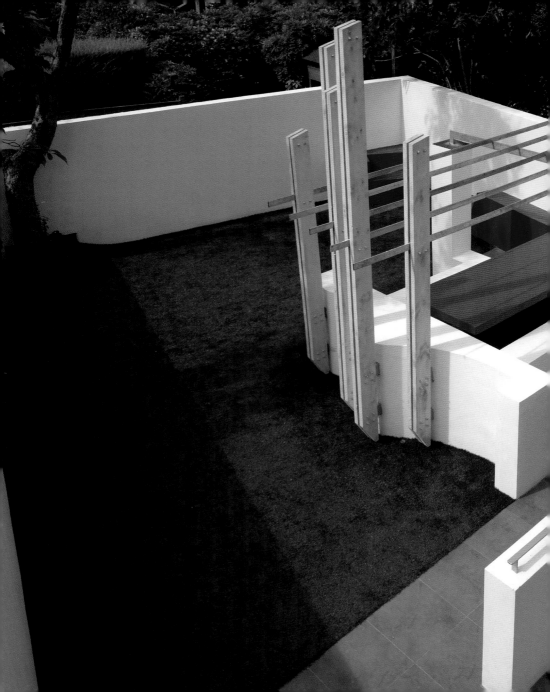

Pergola

Simon Gill, the architect who designed this garden, was given a brief to transform a pretty standard back garden into a low-maintenance garden that fits with a new extension, that would withstand use by children and wouldn't be too costly.

Before

What he decided to do was to 'concentrate the money' on a wonderful steel and concrete structure, a beautiful place to sit and a really unusual focal point for the garden which fits in perfectly with the work Simon has done inside the house.

When you're transforming a garden it's worth thinking about this route, concentrating all your effort and cash on one spectacular thing in the garden – a statue, a water feature or a pergola. If you are going this way, leave the rest of the garden completely minimalist so you don't distract from the show. If this garden had normal flower beds around and climbers, the effect of the structure would be immeasurably lessened. Plants, the things which create the work, would actually have made the garden worse in this case. Instead Simon has concentrated on good design – the rest of the garden looks clean and simple. The walls have been rendered and painted white. The entire effect is to make the uprights of the structure stand out and give a great backdrop to the mauve of the seat.

It's also worth thinking about artificial grass. The clients here have children so the garden needs to be robust enough to take their ball games. The walls and the fake grass are just right to withstand the worst that the children can throw at them.

Garden Plan

The main view into the garden, from the sitting room, has been kept clear with a view down to the tree; the structure is tucked away to the side, to be discovered once you are out in the garden and to make the most of the sunniest spot in the garden.

On the floor is grass – fake grass, the perfect low-maintenance addition to any garden.

Simon Gill, the architect who designed this garden, has used modern materials to make an amazing structure in this garden to give a focal point to the 'room'.

Underneath the pergola is a built-in table and chairs. The table is painted an eye-catching mauve so it shines out against the white walls.

The structure is made of galvanised steel and wood. Its lines follow the lines of the light well – at a slight angle to the house to catch as much light as possible for the below-ground kitchen.

It was important to have the walls of the room perfect and perfectly in keeping with the design – they are a crucial part of this minimalist look, so Simon has rendered and painted them to give a completely clean canvas for the garden. This immediately gives a whole new feel to the garden.

▶ From inside the house, the clean walls of the garden appear to be a continuation of the inside walls.

▲ A concrete wall screens off the sitting area from the rest of the garden.

▼ Fake grass has been used on the floor – the perfect low-maintenance solution for a garden.

▶ Wooden and steel uprights make geometric patterns and cast shadows across the walls.

▲ A line of containers adds greenery to the view out from the house and it's pretty much the only planting in the garden – the exact equivalent of pot plants in an inside room.

▼A huge canvas of plain, painted wall like this is perfect to catch shadows and to watch them as they change through the day and through the season.

▲ The wooden uprights rise well above the metal cross bars to give a sculptural feel to the structure and take it in to the realms of art.

▶ The tree makes wonderful shadows across the built-in seat and the walls.

◀ A light on the wall falls onto a container of planting below, there's also a strip light under the table which makes the table look like it's floating at night.

Meadow planting

This is a very easy garden. It's easy on the eye, easy to live with and, once you've got the design right, it's not too difficult to create one like this. The clients here wanted a low-maintenance garden which flowed naturally from the interior of the house. They wanted a space that they could use all year round with somewhere to eat outside and relax in.

The design was done by Ann Pearce and she has carefully divided the space into three parts with well-proportioned rooms at each end. Near the house is a sitting area with slate shale on the ground and at the rear a sitting area with wooden boards on the ground.

Between them is a wide pathway through planted beds. There's a real feeling of a journey down the garden and, when you are sitting at the rear looking back towards the house through the planting, you feel like you are in the country.

But by keeping the planting to the two beds, Ann has kept the maintenance low. Also by using meadow plants and late flowering perennials she has made the upkeep of the garden a once-a-year affair. In spring all the owners need to do is to go over the two beds with a pair of shears and then wait a few weeks for the plants to start to show through again.

In the winter, the dead seedheads may look glorious if they stay standing and catch the frost. If, however, they fall it might be worth cutting back the plants to ground before the spring.

Garden Plan

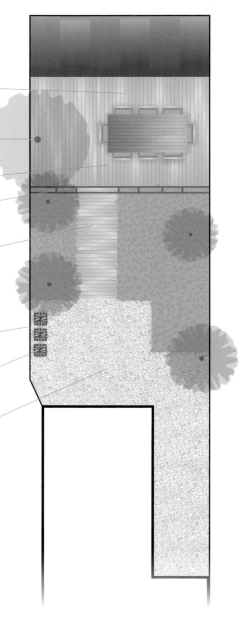

With the planting to one side and walls on the other two, this sitting area feels secluded and hidden away from the world.

The garden is very shady in summer with trees overhanging much of the far end.

At the rear the room's floor is decking.

Wooden uprights form an implied enclosure around the rear area.

The long thin garden has been divided into two rooms with a central pathway between them. There's no lawn in the garden – this makes the maintenance lower and works better in this shady spot.

The brickwork to either side of the garden is the original Victorian red bricks and above these walls bamboo screens give added privacy.

A line of three pots with architectural plants is used to decorate this wall.

The room directly outside the house has slate shale on the floor and plants surrounding it. The slate echoes the slate floors inside the house.

▶ The wooden structure doesn't have overhead elements – it's not there to shade the rear of the garden but to divide the rear area off and give architecture and height to the garden's layout.

▲ Making the most of the shade, there's a hammock hidden at the end of the garden, slung off the wooden uprights.

▲ Because the planting has been kept mainly to these two beds the garden is very low maintenance. There's also no grass to cut.

▲ In the two beds, Ann has planted meadow plants – an abundant mixture which comes into its own in high summer. It's a low-maintenance option for plants – all that needs to be done is to cut them all down either in autumn or the following spring. There are also lots of spring bulbs in here for colour earlier in the year.

◄ The decking isn't decking wood but treated softwood. It gives a more natural feel, less harsh than grooved decking boards or sophisticated hardwoods.

▼ Three enormous bush flax stand in pots on the patio. They are large enough to make a real impact and, as they're so big, their maintenance needs are less and they like being in this shady spot.

▲ In this relaxed garden style it's fine for a cat to take a nap on the plants.

▶ The uprights surrounding the sitting area hold climbing plants like vines.

▼ A grape vine climbs up the posts and gives a Mediterranean feeling to the secluded sitting area.

▼ Geraniums are perfect for a shady garden like this, easy to look after, happy in the shade.

Tiny

I t would be difficult to make a garden of this size high maintenance. In a space 3m by 4m there's a limit to how much you can do, but this garden is a wonderful and exciting use of a small space and it fits in perfectly with the main idea of this book – you don't have to have plants in a garden to make it beautiful!

Before

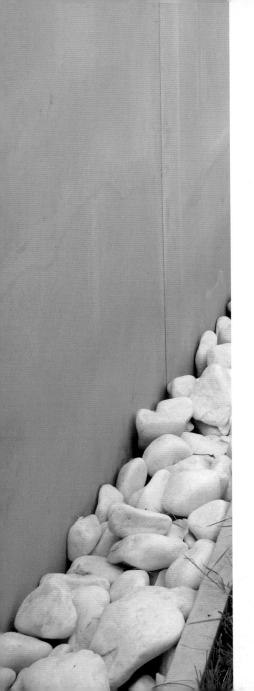

The space was designed by the owner, architect Simon Gill. He has defined a space within the garden with an oblong of grass and added interest to the minimalist composition by incorporating a unique water feature.

Making a feature yourself is a great way to get the perfect object. This one is made of concrete and if you want concrete, you'll need to employ a specialist to make up the feature. Another option is to use fibreglass; again you'll need a specialist fabricator to make it up for you from your drawings.

My favourite part of the water feature is the shallow pool which sits directly outside the sitting room door; it is clever and quirky and brings the water right into the house with its reflections.

The only plant life in the garden is the grass. It's an important feature, giving a green plane all through the year and setting off the light bright marble and limestone around it. But it could just as easily be artificial grass reducing the maintenance further.

Garden Plan

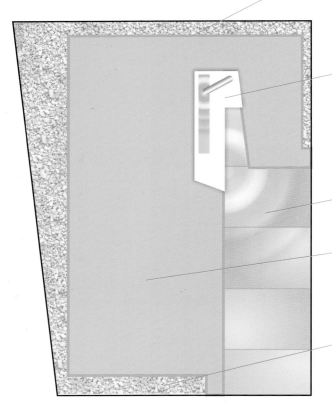

Even though the garden is tiny, Simon has still made his own shape within the space – the line of the grass doesn't follow the line of the wall. Instead it makes a good regular oblong lined up with the house.

The main feature of the garden is a water feature designed by Simon; it is made from concrete with a stainless-steel spout.

This limestone area is part of the water feature – it forms a shallow pool which reflects sunlight up into the house.

The grass is really the only maintenance issue here, and the owner and designer of the garden, architect Simon Gill, is probably going to replace it with artificial grass to cut down the maintenance still further.

There are three materials on the floor. Tumbled marble cobbles for a white bright effect. Grass for all-year-round greenery and limestone for a smooth and sleek look to the base of the pool.

▶ The water feature is made from poured concrete. A stainless-steel spout pours water down a rill and out into the pool.

▲ At one end a shelf hides outlet pipes.

▶ The water feature was designed by the owner, architect Simon Gill. This channel is made from concrete which has been 'bush hammered', basically knocked about with an uneven hammer to give it a rough texture. Why? So the water trickles and sparkles down the channel rather than running smoothly.

▼ For once the neighbours' greenery is adding to the composition. These fronds hanging over the fence make a pretty pattern against the sleek white wall.

▼ The water in the pool has been cleverly designed to cast reflections up into the rooms inside the house, so sunshine dances on the ceiling.

Classic

This is the sort of garden that has wide appeal, the design manages to stay on that delicate line between modern and traditional; it has a great deal of style but not so much that you are afraid to go into it. The owners wanted a garden that looked good all year round and matched the interior which they have opened out for a modern feel, yet have used traditional materials in keeping with the period house.

The garden was designed by Sara Jane Rothwell of Glorious Gardens and she has used a light touch here to create a classic yet modern garden fitting perfectly with the interior.

The patio is a great example of this. Sara Jane has pushed back the lower level to provide a wide usable space for a table and chairs, but rather than create a square she has tapered the patio round towards the steps. So instead of a simple, starkly modern rectangular patio, it steps inward to the rear to give interest to the shape. The walls are rendered but rather than leave the render with just paint on it, as modern style would demand, she has topped it off with light-coloured sandstone. It looks clean and contemporary but also very easy to live with.

With the stepping stones in the lawn, a purely traditional view would have these in random sizes and laid in a curve, but Sara Jane has laid them dead straight and used regular geometric square slabs.

With all of this, the owners have a garden that's easy to live with and in many ways that is the secret of a low-maintenance garden. Yes, there are easy-to-look-after evergreen plants in here; and, yes, there's a really strong structure which helps. But there's also a softness which means that if there are a few leaves on the lawn here it doesn't matter – it's not so stark as to show up the slightest imperfection in its maintenance.

8

Garden Plan

The garden has been pushed back to create a large usable space outside the house enclosed by low retaining walls.

The owners of the garden wanted to keep a lawn for its softness and all-year-round greenery.

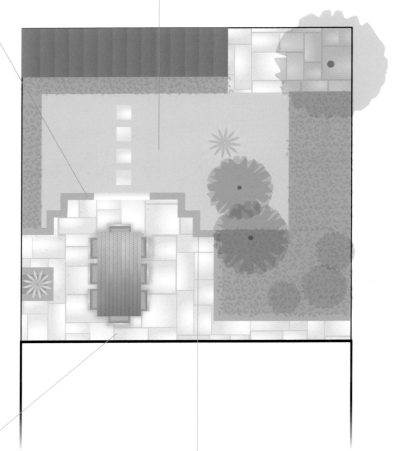

The house and the garden have been designed together so there is a seamless flow between garden room and terrace.

Around the sides of the patio, rendered walls fit in perfectly with the modern/traditional style of the house. They are rendered and painted a lovely modern light colour, but capped with sandstone for a more traditional feel.

▶ It is amazing to think that there is nothing of any height in the garden; the structure is very clear and well defined, just by using low growing plants, paths and stones.

◀ Paving stones sunk into the turf form a path. Again these have good strong modern lines but also have a traditional feel which is in keeping with the house and the rest of the garden. The stones are set below the grass so the mower can ride right over them.

▼ Bulbs are great for giving seasonal colour without much work. Up they come year after year – the only big effort is when you have to plant them.

▲ Around the base of a tree the low-maintenance solution is to put down cobbles and pebbles to stop weeds coming up but allow water through.

▼ Random-laid York stone blocks with brick edging of London stock give clean bright lines yet a traditional look to the garden. The low box hedges provide greenery without causing too much work.

Containers

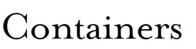

This is an interesting garden to look at. When the photos were taken it had literally just been finished, so the design of the garden is still raw and it's easy to see all of the lines before they are softened by planting.

James Lee, the designer here, has used quality materials to get a simple and elegant garden. The decking pathway is made of balau hardwood – more expensive than softwood but its quality shines out. If you want a path going right down the garden it's going to be quite a major element of the design and it pays to make it a thing of beauty.

James has used the budget for the garden wall – rather than have the hardwood trellis over all the walls James has used it only where it will show in the long term, elsewhere the walls will be covered with planting. It's a really good idea if you want a beautiful wood but don't want to break the bank by putting it on all the walls.

He has also made sure that the garden is easy to look after. All the planting is contained in quite small but incredibly well-defined beds. Over two-thirds of the garden is either hard landscaping or grass, but by using tall plants and climbers James has made the most of the screening and covering properties of plants grown in quite narrow beds and containers.

9

Garden Plan

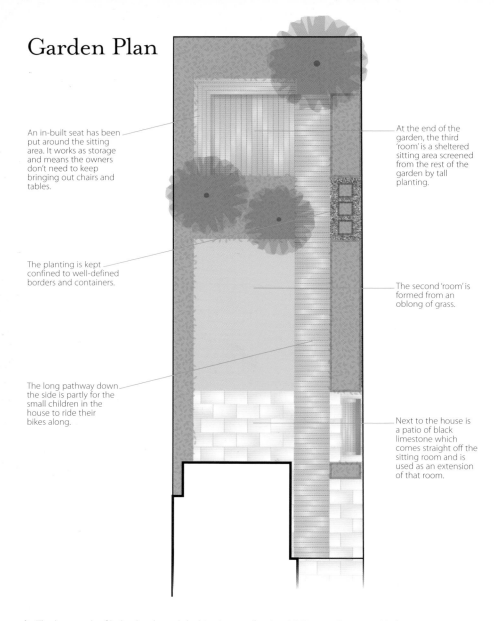

An in-built seat has been put around the sitting area. It works as storage and means the owners don't need to keep bringing out chairs and tables.

The planting is kept confined to well-defined borders and containers.

The long pathway down the side is partly for the small children in the house to ride their bikes along.

At the end of the garden, the third 'room' is a sheltered sitting area screened from the rest of the garden by tall planting.

The second 'room' is formed from an oblong of grass.

Next to the house is a patio of black limestone which comes straight off the sitting room and is used as an extension of that room.

▶ The long path of balau hardwood decking is great for the children to play on and helps to maintain a sense of the length of this garden. James used 140mm width boards rather than the normal 90mm boards to get the proportions right.

◀ A cantilevered bench is perfectly proportioned against the slatted panel behind.

▲ These modern panels will, when the garden is mature, be the only parts of the fence that are really visible and will help to give a really contemporary feel to the garden. They are made of western red cedar.

▲ The cantilevered seat is enclosed by planters which jut out into the garden.

▼ At the rear of the garden James has painted the back fence a light colour (Borrowed Light by Farrow & Ball) to help brighten up the area and break up the line of red/brown fences.

▲ From the house you can see how well the garden matches the inside of the house. The lines of low planters outside continue the line of low cupboards inside. The colours, too, are well matched, the planters outside are galvanised steel, powder-coated in red from Gardens and More Ltd.

▶ The children's planters are for them to grow vegetables. They've been coloured to match the units inside the kitchen.

◀ Easy-to-look-after plants like these Russian sages will grow to fill out the planters.

9

Raised beds

10

If your back garden is just a rectangle of earth surrounded by an assortment of fences, look at this and take heart. If anything the view here was worse than most – there's an enormous wall at the bottom of the garden, keeping out light and dominating the space. This garden was just a bare room with tall walls.

Before

The owners wanted a practical, child-friendly garden which was easy to maintain, but how to get there? They realised a major overhaul was necessary and brought in the garden designer Pamela Johnson.

One thing she has done wonderfully well here is to introduce interest without making work. The lawn went and was replaced by sleek black limestone slabs – an immediate time saver. The side walls have been rendered and painted a light colour to look modern but also to lighten the whole area, and along all the walls raised beds have been built.

This is a great solution if your garden has overpowering walls – raised beds cut down that flat plane of wall and they also introduce plants into the garden in a delightfully easy-to-look-after way. Pamela has used large specimen plants because they fit the style of the garden, but also because they look great all year round and pretty much look after themselves.

The overall effect is a stylish garden but an interesting and green one too. There are built-in seats and the splendid pond to really draw you into the space and make it work for the whole family.

Garden Plan

Architectural plants are used because they are low maintenance; they give great year-round colour and their structure brilliantly complements the architecture around them.

There's no lawn in the garden – this immediately reduces the amount of maintenance needed. A sweep down every once in a while is all this garden needs.

Raised beds also lessen the impact of the surrounding walls by hiding the lower half of the wall.

Halfway down the garden is a hook for a child's tent to be hung from.

On each side of the garden there is a gap in the raised bed and an in-built seat. If the light coloured line of the raised bed went all the way down it would be too overpowering and a line leading right down the garden would make the space look thinner and shorter. This gap breaks that line and brings a widening influence to the design.

Using raised beds helps to make the plants more manageable and more contained. The soil, brought into the garden to fill these beds, can be guaranteed weed free.

The water feature makes good use of the tall rear wall and turns what could have been a negative element into a positive benefit to the garden.

▶ The garden is full of plants, but big ones. These tall, architectural plants need very little looking after and fill the garden without making it fussy.

▲ Both the side walls have been rendered and painted the same colour and topped off with horizontal battens to give a unified look. Fences have been finished in modern horizontal slats and uprights have been brought down the wall to give a great architectural detail. (The very tall rear wall has been left as open brick – if it had been painted a flat, light colour it would have jumped forward and overpowered the garden.)

▲ Black limestone, laid in a regular pattern, has been used on the floor. This is sawn and so the finish is sleek and smooth rather than the uneven surface of riven limestone.

◀ The raised beds don't have trailing plants which would be too wispy for this garden but some of the plants do come over the side to make architectural shapes against the cream walls.

▶ The fish pond uses the rear wall to get a fall of water over black limestone platforms which makes a great sound in the garden.